TALES FROM ANOTHER ME

A COLLECTION OF WORKS BY HAYDEN GRIBBLE

Copyright © Hayden Gribble 2006-2010, 2015, 2020

Cover illustration copyright © John Galantini 2015

First published by Amazon Kindle in February 2015

This version published by Lightning Source 2020

All rights reserved

The moral rights of the author have been asserted

The right of Hayden Gribble to be identified as the author of this work has been asserted by him in accordance with the Copyright, Designs and Patents Act 1988.

This book is sold subject to the condition that it shall not, by way of trade or otherwise, be lent, resold, hired out or otherwise circulated without the publisher's prior written consent in any form of binding or cover other than that in which it is published and without a similar condition including this condition being imposed on the subsequent purchaser.

ISBN 978-1-9998659-4-8

Printed and bound by Lightning Source

www.haydengribble.net

CONTENTS

Foreword
Acknowledgements

The Protective Blanket
Awakening
A New Dawn
Untitled#1
Butterfingers
Skin Deep in Mid Sleep
Clockwork Doll
Solution to the Problem
Same Sun, Different Skies
Ventilator
Looking Up at the Sky
Queen of the Fairies
Gone But Not Forgotten
Silverspoon Paradise
Only Human
Hazy Days
Listen To Me
A Bond That Was Made To Be Broken
Someone Lost A Generation
Intercity Observation
The Academic Jesters
Watchers of the Sky
Silver Sparks
Do You Like It?
Our Stories Are Left by the Chapters we leave Behind
Untitled#2
Splutter
Swings and Roundabouts
Never Gone
Last Man of his Kind
Synapse
My Life Through Your Eyes (written with Simon Dymond)
Clouds of Thunder
Skyscraping
Fall

Afterword

FOREWORD

I hope you enjoy my angst-ridden scribblings.

Proceeds from this book will be donated to Mind UK.

Hayden Gribble

This book is dedicated to the main players in my life at the time that these poems were written.

You're all in here, somewhere.

The Protective Blanket

Ball bearing bullets shatter your windscreen
A protective blanket when killing the speed
These soldiers of freedom hasten your safety
Despite being peaceful there weapon is hate
Open your eyes you can see through the curtains
The serpent is calling you through the cracks in your wardrobe
Enticing you to call out the names you've forgotten
Of the people who made you who you are today
Do we break down the borders we made in the decades?
The way we were before listening to radio waves
That chalk on our fingers reminds us who's slipping
Down the rope that keeps us so neatly tied together

Awakening

Building blocks for the future in the kingdom of grey
Say goodbye to the masses in the pouring rain
Well society crumbles and it's bringing you down
How the mighty have fallen when they're teeth hit the ground
And the shapes of their egos as the wall collides
Stopping people in their tracks, slowly morph into flies
A superpower is broken someone fit the mould
Before the man you trusted steals all you behold
Because nothings the same as yesterday
If we were too happy then we'd go insane
Without problems dilemmas float away
To an island of some known castaway
Nervous and anxious, those emotions occur

When two people have fallen into wars of words
Machine guns and bullets are the only way
That our nation's leaders can negotiate
Because nothings the same as yesterday
If we were too happy then we'd go insane
Without problems dilemmas float away
To an island of some known castaway
We're always slipping and sliding
Testifying, testify against the morals of foes
Repress your feelings, help the needy
Helping your friends is what matters the most
But when you lack the patients
Sack the patients, slack of patience
Headaches make you moan
But when it comes to survival
Consult the manual
You can't let this moment get in your way

A New Dawn

Good news, good times
The wall of climbing frames
A treacherous path, no longer starved
Of a pleasure I'm going to gain

Sweet sixteen, summer draws near
Out with the paper in with the beer
Holding the flag high, triumphant I cry
The next steps just begun.....

No need for money
No need to try
For the rest of the moment
I want to ride the tide

Untitled#1

Glass prisms dance in the blue and red
Splinters of old news prickle your cold heart
Turquoise satellite dishes hits the purple
Natures got itself another hurdle
Whispers they hail down through autumn leaves
The words carried through the weekend retreats
You better be careful on the zebra crossing today
As the man whose driving might look the other way

Snowy English hills in mid may
Thinking the ice age could be kicking in
Dangerous streets at midnight we walk along
Dangerous deeds we are witnessing day by day
Light box shimmering in my eyes
Beams that make my blood pressure rise
Help my brain blossom into something new
And days away in the morning dew

Butterfingers

Stories sworn to secrecy
Lips I mustn't touch
A blot on my brain
Telling me to watch what I say

Casually passing the deceivers
Of yesterdays dreamers
They want to fill my head
With sharp petal leaves and snowflakes

I won't have it anyway
It's just another story
About forgotten glory
The devils way of playing his game

Judging books by their covers
With their spines so crooked
Like the landscapes they create
Another casualty to add to the slate

Corridors with dead ends cornering you
inside

The deck has been dealt and you have the joker
They pack you right in and make you a puppet
There's no other way out, and there's no way to stop it
Push through the holes
Harden up on the outside
Follow your morals and don't hide your pride
Look out for the kneaders
The company feeders
Hide away your butterfingers
I hope you can fix this in time

Skin Deep in Mid Sleep

Something washing over me
Walking through my heart and soul
Bury my hands in this awkward sand
I need to find a more conscious land

Differences are far away
Please come back another day
Take my hand, this is too easy
All this sentiment makes me queasy

Protected from constricting chains
Before my memory misbehaves
Take me back to the good old days
When mind expanding was all the rave

When Saturday morning comes
I'll be screaming out my lungs
All these toxins floating around my body
The countries way of acting bawdy

Holidays melting in fun
The winter melted by sun

Our fellow people will run
Insults seem to slip off our tongues
Always lurking in the dark
A young man wants to make a mark
Follow your instinct smite the greedy
Saying 'I want the people to see me'

Holidays melting in fun
The winter melted by sun
Our fellow people will run
Insults seem to slip off our tongues

Clockwork Doll

Nasty surprises await you my dear
Don't say I didn't warn you
When the walls are closing in
And the floor disappears from below your feet

Your dizzy head's on the block
About to join the traitors on the spike
You've run out of options, and shoulders to cry on
Like a lamb to the slaughter you are

I was always your clockwork doll
You'd wind me up just to watch me fall
You'd cover me in paint just to watch me stick
To the shoes you made me kiss

Mouthwash is meant to make you clean
It melted away your poisonous words
You've dodged those bullets a million times before

But mines the one that will get you

I was always your clockwork doll
You'd wind me up just to watch me fall
You'd cover me in paint just to watch me stick
To the shoes you made me kiss
Did you get away from this?
Without suffering the consequences

Have you twisted your letters again?
To spell a word from which you gain

I was always your clockwork doll
You'd wind me up just to watch me fall
You'd cover me in paint just to watch me stick
To the shoes you made me kiss

Solution to the Problem

Life kicks us in the teeth
And we all have the fillings to prove it
It's only a quick release, an excuse to be
young and foolish
But will it catch me in the end?
Ambition drives me on
I hope I don't forget who I leave behind
Do we fight the greed? Or hunger for the
need?
Barrels down the hill
Water under the bridge
Falling in love with someone you miss
We run that risk
Come out of the water
There's no need for restrain
If only I could hold the moment
Just to keep me sane
Darkness whips across the faces
Of all who celebrate the downfall of success

Same Sun, Different Skies

Glints of ice beams in cherry coloured eyes
Tinted that way to disguise your starry night
The black holes of time, eclipsing sunrise
Boarding up pain, blocking out the grain
Of seas of adventures in outer space flourish
Across the wilderness which slips through your fingers
And dines on the grass with a warm thermos flask
A pool of waves and torrent leave your troubles behind
Light shines out of the satisfaction your spreading
And sleep like fairy dust falls from your sockets
Ignoring the world for what it really is
An emotionless struggle to leave the abyss
And come and explore new chapters being born
With a soul flying high like doves in the sky
But spangles like moonlight shot rain
No longer attacked by the other mammals

Verbally and physically ignoring it all when
Bitten hard by molars like teeth in a comb
But the bloods filled with rainbows
As floating on florescent clouds
So soft and white, the moons got it right
Looking down on the chaos below him
And I don't blame him for hiding from us
You don't need rockets to shoot to the stars
You just need a notepad, inhaler and a heavy heart

Ventilator

Felt like fingers in sun beaten jean pockets
Brain nourished by facts that won't get me anywhere
But make me feel proud of what I've achieved

Great Britain's just a name to days gone by
We and our peers are the next dreamers
Passing the torch on through generations
Until we're happy with what we preach to future relations

More colourful than the brightest rainbow
A future through kaleidoscope telescopes
Wheels of fortune
Make or break decisions
Ripples that skim the river forever
And people's bridges just keep on building

Gazing up from a country cornfield
The crop engulfing my resistance of normality

Let the birds whisper me sweet nothings
again
Because that's all they ever do to taunt me

The stars keep changing colours
Zipping across the blanket of darkness
My new coat makes me look triangular
In the moonlight shadows

There's another revolution waiting to happen

<u>Looking Up at the Sky</u>

You wouldn't believe me
But the sky is swirling
In front of me
Lying in a field
Not knowing who to talk to
Or what to see

The sky is changing
Colours again
Red, gold and orange
My perfect ten
My dreams are in the clouds
Looking up at the sky

And I can feel
The world turning
And I can feel
The ether burning
And I can smell
The aroma of freedom
Engulfing me

If I close my eyes
The magic goes
And it burns into my brain
As I ride this train
It's so beautiful
There is so much to be seen
Of the place I so wish I could have been

And I can feel
The world turning
And I feel
The acid working
And I can sense
The stormy weather
About to overtake me

And I can feel
The world turning
And I can feel
The planet burning
And I can smell
The sunshine approaching
Looking up at the sky

Queen of the Fairies

I know a girl who's clueless to how she behaves
Crippled at birth by the monsters she makes

She keeps herself locked inside her bitterness and sorrow
And love for her has been a bitter pill to swallow

She thinks she's queen of the fairies
When she's really lord of the flies

But her loneliness is just a disguise
She's waiting for the smile that could melt a thousand hearts

Forever experiencing regretful episodes
Sleeping with people just as shallow as her

Always saying 'I will follow my heart
And my head will follow later'
About those sorry men

Who didn't want to see her?

Until she meets the man
In the same boat as she is in
Going along the same lonely water

There's a million to one chance they will meet
So until that day she'll just have to grit her teeth
And as the years and enamel fall away
She'll have to find another way to play her game

Gone But Not Forgotten

Someone watching over me
Walking through my heart and soul
Making me feel warm inside
Without them I'd fall and cry

Names they burn inside of me
Each one with a memory
As life bears down on me
I slowly lose my identity

I'm trapped
I'm trapped within this time
Let me go
Let me go

Show me the way to go
Show me the way to get out of here

Hunger is the enemy
Of the slaves of mutiny
Your ageing face is looking grim
Taking defeat on the chin

Said the father to the son
Life has only just begun
The path you take will decide
What you become on the other side

Looking back into the past
I see the light that broke my eyes
The memories you left behind
Will serve me well when I leave this time

Silverspoon Paradise

As I lie on the floor
Dusty fan swings above the door
Thinking this could all mean something

Mountains of boxes in front of my eyes
Towered so high they make the ceiling rise
Processions like profits mean nothing to me

Is this how you like to live your life?
In a silverspoon paradise
When you don't have to labour for the things you keep
Because mummy and daddy have you under lock and key

Pins in the wood keep the paper still
For the messages that explain the hours to kill
A way to document how to spend your time

Wasting away brain cells in a specific way
Bring a close to another day
In which there is too much time to sacrifice

Is this how you like to live your life?
In a silverspoon paradise
When you don't have to labour for the things you keep
Because mummy and daddy have you under lock and key

Only Human

The world gives us life
Are we giving anything back?

Are we trying to be adults?
Or looking into things too much

Disillusioned by the things we see
There's no such thing as independency

As we are always needy
For other people's things, we are too greedy

Are we sure of giving up instead of going to try
Before the idea pales and inspiration dies

It's okay because everybody cries
But aren't you scared of the day we die?

Nothing lasts forever, we should accept that now
Day by day something's changed, how?

Whether its mood, money or the people we love
Or the way the world is run by the people above

The world gives us life
Are we giving anything back?
Because if we're looking for days of judgement
We're all going to crack

Hazy Days

Engulfed in dense pockets of clouds round my mind

Different colours, shaped differently in these wide eyes

Floating in a tide like a breeze through a corn field

Brighter and wilder and the objects I yield

Hazy days are these
When you can see rainbow rings around the moon
And shadows of people that come and go,
That feeling happens all too soon

Warm soft sunlight creates my tones
A feeling that tells us we're never alone
Nursery rhymes all a haze
In a nod to our more venerable days

Addiction is the key, the thing we crave
To the chemicals that make us misbehave

Stuck in between consciousness and wild reality
I sleep in the past and awake in the future

Hazy days are these
When you can see rainbow rings around the moon
And the shadows of people come and go
And that feeling happens all too soon

Listen To Me

Shall we get this meeting started?
Are you prepared?
Are you going to listen to me?
Or pretend you're not here?

I hope you take in what I'm about to say
If not, your making a big mistake
Are you going to listen to me?
Or pretend you're somewhere else?

Bubbles like blisters form on your memory
And give you a sense of false reality
Life's made up with brave decisions
And yours are ruling out your possibilities

You've become stuck in limbo
Between consciousness and the real world
And I hate to say it
But you will never fit in our mould

Better to leave now before you get
Washed away in envy

We're very different people you and I
The methods you preach should be fused away
Last chance saloon closed for good
We don't want you here disobeying me
But this I'll say before you leave on this day
Is that you brought the burden
and lowered your own curtain

A Bond That Was Made To Be Broken

Crushing the anthill with your barefoot
You always had an appetite for destruction
didn't you?

Are you scared you won't fit in?
Resort to the comfort of fake smiles and grins

Your telling lies which turn into reality
What bides between us is slowly breaking
down
Real friends never want to hurt you that are
true
Looking back makes me realise
The umbrella of peace is closed for good

In years from now will you still be sore
From experiences of old
And forever in the past

Looking back through eyes
That appears unforgiving
In a world that's made for living

Are you making a difficult decision easy?
Or being selfish when protecting
Yourself from the harm of others

And leaving your frame of mind
In a bid to be unkind

I can't be there in your hour of need
A bond which was made to be broken
You've already committed the deed

Someone Lost A Generation

She's been for a drive
Seen all the sites
Of the beautiful people

Her thoughts have been slain
Crashed in the lane
Car blew away her pride

Blue in the mouth
There's something about
The way she turns to greet them

Is your life a mess?
How could I guess?
Wash your hands completely

Nobody knows, just how it goes
Where's your four leafed clover?
Cradle the sand, head in your hands
Trying to win things over

Confidence slain
Life in the fast lane

Is not all it's meant to be

Slam on the brakes
The screeching of rakes
Rips her up completely

She went too far
Spirits, cigars
In bed with anyone easy

She's hooked on the hard stuff
Up the nose stuff
Let this be a warning

Nobody knows, just how it goes
Where's your four leafed clover?
Cradle the sand, head in your hands
Trying to win things over

Intercity Observation

Did you see them on the train?
Fighting like boxers swapping punches
Each one fighting to be heard
But none of whom win the contest

Look at the people walking by
Imagine knowing what makes them cry
Hustle and bustle of time drifting by
Each one with dreams of days gone dry

Taxi lights burn my head
Bet they wish that I were dead
That balding man behind the wheels
At weekends takes too many pills
Did you see them in the cafe?
Reaching quantities of gingersnaps
Talking to their loved ones
Spilling coffee all over their clothes

When Saturday morning comes
I'll be screaming out my lungs
I won't want to be here

Because these streets I call my own suit me better

The Academic Jesters

Shall we see how far we can push them?
Who can get away with the most?
Tag team brothers pissing the day away
We can't wait till the end of the game

What's so wrong with a little fun?
Don't you remember when you were young?
When you joked about the day
And wondered what the people really say?

Your child won't go far if he doesn't listen
He talks to much, and tries to take charge
We moved him away from his friend today
But that didn't stop there comedic ways

Your childish self has given up turning
Up to face the day
If your son doesn't buck up his ideas
He won't be allowed to stay

What's so wrong with a little fun
Don't you remember when you were young

When you joked about the day
And wondered what the people really say?
He's in his own world, we've given up trying
We'll see what summer brings
And hopefully for us he'll spread his wings

Watchers of the Sky

The morning came and the lights went out
And the people from the south danced about
And those empty skies and those hollow hearts
Melted away this week's horoscope
The flowers in bloom now falling down
As they discover what today is all about
It's time to put things right
We're the watchers of the sky
The hungry wolves chase the city signs
And the others are left with a clouded mind
What we borrow we keep but can't let go
This is how we'll feel in a month or so
The clouds will part and the dogs are musting
Armies of lovers soul discovering
I hope that I will change
I can never stay the same
It's a new dawn
But I'm falling again
We're going backwards to how we came in the first place
From the oceans

From the trees
My worlds in motion
The flaming trees and those swollen eyes
The stars swoop down
The lamps just shine
On through a glaze of morning fog
Some of us will just keep watching the skies

Silver Sparks

Venture forward looking back
Forever stuck in the cal-de-sac
Sink or swim our inner thoughts
Tucked away in creaking draws
Concrete blocks paralyse my feet
As I chase the light that leaves the room
Embers of the past burn away
It's good to look forward in a nervous way
Wolf packs hound the weekend walkers
Like tigers the prowl through a swollen heart
Venture forward looking back
Forever stuck in your cal-de-sac

Do You Like It?

Do you like it when the empty Sunday morning comes?
Would you like to have fun just like anyone?

When you're down in the dumps and there's a man on your back
Saying, "listen son, you've just got to bounce back!"

Would you like to be free from the perils and strife?
That's an added bonus to your modern life?

Would you like to look back and say let's start again
Before the voices of doubt crept inside your head?

No I won't leave you this way
I'm going to sit this one out
No, I can't bear you this way
I'm going to sit this one out

Do you like it when the fears for yourself will arise?
A secret which leaves you broken, surprised!

There are many people, put yourself in their shoes
Shall I go and tell him my impending news?

Would you take me seriously if I lived in a flat?
Sitting here in my jester hat?

It may surprise you that my sympathies gone
Since you ripped out the place where my trust belongs

No I'm going to leave here today
I'm going to sit this one out
Can I presume, this is the final kiss
I wanted to sit this one out

Our Stories Are Left By the Chapters we leave

Gazing out of windows
That don't show you all you should see
The wanderer has had his day
The stranger doesn't want to play
Dreams stop us from getting bored while we sleep
And make our everyday paths more bearable

The race we are should yield the fact
That our minds are full of junk, that's that
And the alarm bells start to sound
As the king hands down his age old crown
He doesn't like what he sees down the human timeline

The older generation always thinks
The successors get in the way
There's another revolution waiting to happen they explain
But it's just the same as their father's decade
As they get carried away

With the garden emporiums they make

Reminding them from where they came
And remembering that on Sunday it always rains
Restricting themselves with careers and families
And stabilise themselves with hair dye and money
Whilst there young ones they choose to fight
The everyday parasites
Who've woven into the social fabric?
And stop you from believing

And when you hit that common age
That's when you're filled with jealousy and hate
That your young ones are so grown up now
And have the chance to do what you didn't do
That's grab life by both hands
And not give up just because you're forty-two

Untitled#2

Timber Shakes
Fairy cakes
Freshly baked
Glasses shingle
Fingers tingle
Early rise
Late demise
Fires flaming
Plastic melting
Glue becoming undone
A friendly one-to-one
Unearthly smells
The gates of hell
Sand dunes rolling
Nine to five tolling
Higher stakes
Cheese grates
Jaguar purrs
Sleepy head stirs
Memory bank stores
The urge for a whole lot more

Splutter

We search for treasure
We're on the hunt
We stand under heaters to get away from the cold

We ask for directions
When all hope looks lost
And we wake up on Monday morning to work for our boss

We look to the past
When we're done with the present

We look to our tasks
With glee for our future

We chase the pigeons out of our sheds
When all we want is to go back to our nests

Swings and Roundabouts

Sooth the burn
The pain is in reserve
For mistakes we make
And people we hate
Snap the coil
We've seen too much
Are we spoiling the day?
Running away
Got to find a new release
Got to protect the words we speak
The flavours fade away
From the fruits we made today
They'll be forgotten again
Trampled into the ground
Rocks on the mountains
Are quietly falling down
We're unstoppable again
Throwing our weight around
Silence me
Stop me falling off
The wheels again
Build me up again

Never Gone

Littered schemes by go betweens
Frozen lakes from the paths once made
Bring and buy
Take and cry
Exchange of smoke
From the fire that died
Listen to the call on your answer machine
What do we do with our memories?
Exchange what we had
For brick and brack
We're moving on
But you're never gone from me
Take the chill from social skills
The war is won but which are we on
I'm bulletproof from insults hurled at me
I grew a thicker skin
To hide what's within
Listen to the call on your answer machine
What do we do with our memories?
Exchange what we had
For brick and brack
We're moving on

But you're never gone from me

Last Man Of His Kind

Let me tell you the story of a man if I can
He lives his life by the palm of his hand
He sleeps through day just to drink by night
When the morning comes his life is a fight

He sings his song to the charm of the town
His wallet full of kings and crowns
He buys his friends with drink and drugs
The kind he picks up from the local thugs

One of his friends is a criminal thief
Doing jobs for the mafia chief
There's a debt to be paid so his running away
Drives to Dover to escape the exposure

Let me tell you the story of a man if I can
He lives his life by the palm of his hands
He slept through day just to drink by night
When the morning came his soul was a flight

Synapse

It's a common misconception
To be born a saint and to die a devil
And to live your life like there's no tomorrow
And make all the money you can

But all these issues frighten me
This is not the life I want to lead
I'm crying out for being free
Free from the pain and misery

Suburban life is not worth my while
I've had enough of this ride
I have my ghosts, like the most
Of the people who survived

Aspirations suitably high
We thought we could reach the sky
But nowadays the smiles have gone
Been replaced by clouds of storm

I faced the world the world smiled back
Why do I keep stuttering down this track?
The way you live it drives me insane

Like pulling a coat hanger out of my brain

Suburban life is not worth my while
I've had enough of this ride
I have my ghosts, like the most
Of the people who survived

My Life Through Your Eyes _(written with Simon Dymond)_

Hundred million people
Each one with dreams of fame
Living they're lives through government lies
Awake but not alive

Houses like boxes machine made
Each one senseless, numb and decayed
Fields with their names set in stone
Praying to be remembered all unknown

My life through your eyes
A birth a job a death

My life through your eyes
Expiry date set

Dangerous toxic voices
Through a numb black screen
Dominates your home, soon you'll be alone
For a reason home-grown

My life through your eyes

I can see through your eyes

But I don't see a reflection of me
Just a shade of what I've become

Clouds Of Thunder

Table for five
Eaten alive
Blink your eyes
Realise
Going under
Clouds of thunder
Spoil my choice
Break my voice
Stop your noise
Energise
Going under
Clouds of thunder
Sleep well tonight
Through the fright
Buckle under eyes
Paralyse
Going under
Clouds of thunder
Storm comes closer
Run for shelter

Skyscraping

Up among the clouds
Looks are deceiving
Rainclouds are heaving
In the air they crowd
Waiting to explore
All the earth below
I'm shooting our my thoughts again
I'm shooting in the dark again
I should have learnt to run
Before I struggle to breath
Every year in June
I spend my days in the sun
A little light never hurt anyone
But it's over when the evening comes
Waiting to explore
I'm shooting our my thoughts again
I'm shooting in the dark again
I should have learnt to run
Before I struggle to breath

Fall

Where have all the buttercups gone?
Just like the daisies, blown away
Oh how I wish they'd stay another week
Rumbling amongst the hay
Before your loved ones go astray
Sunday ravers, blessed are the meek
Silver clad spiders on the lawn
Little boy blue has blown his horn
Our freedom, days for victory are done
Sailing on a carpet past the moon
God only knows, she's leaving soon
Back to reality, hello mundane life
Because it's all gone
Summer days they should be made for fun
It's all gone
Soon be left to wonder what I've done
Playing out Barrett in my room
Golden haired girl, what a loon
But oh the words, they make sense in my mind
No regrets there telling me
All my dreams went out to sea

Independent, that's what I must be
Because it's all gone
Summer days they should be made for fun
It's all gone
Soon be left to wonder what I've done
So what did I do man
I want to make a stand and join a band
I want to write words to make you laugh and weep
Got to keep hold of your friends
They help with your baggage in the end
When the summer days have turned into rain
Because it's all gone
Summer days they should be made for fun
It's all gone
Soon be left to wonder what I've done

Afterword

Venturing forward, looking back…

Also Available:

Captain Random and the Eater of Souls

ISBN: 978-1999865931

Following their explosive battle with the Sandman, and struggling to come to terms with life out in space, the crew of the Venus II decide to throw themselves into a spot of retail therapy on the friendly planet of Genocia.

But almost as soon as they arrive, they realise that this new world is not all that it seems. Outside the splendour and vast wealth of the Grand Chamber lies a neglected wasteland where terror lurks within the poisonous gloom whilst deep within the bowels of the planet lies a terrible secret.

At the very heart of it all is the ruthless leader Consula, whose designs for supremacy mean ultimate devastation to all of those who oppose her. But the greed and corruption of the government is nothing compared to what lurks in the shadows for Random and his friends. Separated and fighting for their lives, Random, Anji, Jake and Skateboard must work quickly to save the lives of the prisoners stuck in the mines deep below the surface, where death is very close by...

What is the Soul Destroyer? What part does it play in Consula's diabolical plan? Will Anji ever see her friends again? One thing is for sure. The Eater of Souls is hungry...

Captain Random vs the Sandman

ISBN: 978-1999865924

Rodas. The scorned planet of Ursa-17. Ravaged by centuries of war between two factions, the villainous Sapphire Regime and the ruthless Crimson Empire. The reason behind the conflict of red and blue? The people of Rodas were unable to make the colour purple.
Until one day, when two rebels, one from either side, combine to create the ultimate warrior. A being who could put an end to the battle of ages and bring peace to the volatile planet of Rodas once and for all.

There is one tiny drawback. The warrior is a boy.

***** Fantastic book, enjoyed every part of it!
Highly recommend it for Dr Who/Red Dwarf/Rick and Morty fans.

***** Hayden Gribble's writing is witty and clever with an essence of Douglas Adams in there too. Would thoroughly recommend for anyone with an adventurous spirit.

***** I really enjoyed it. I can well imagine Kids getting swept along with the interstellar, action packed adventure and chuckling along with all the funny scenarios and characters and wanting to know just what happens .

Available from all good book shops.

Child Out of Time: Growing Up With Doctor Who in the Wilderness Years

ISBN: 978-1999865900

For 26 years, DOCTOR WHO was a British institution, capturing the imaginations of generations of children. But then, in 1989, it was cancelled. The Doctor and his on-screen adventures were no more. There was no longer a hero, a champion for the outcasts who struggled to fit in. It was as though he had walked into his TARDIS and set his controls for dematerialisation, never to return: a whole generation lost to the powers of Science Fiction's greatest creation. It was in this Doctor-less world that I grew up. This is the story of how one little boy would try to find the Doctor in any way, shape or form and the obstacles he faced in doing so. This is the story of growing up without Doctor Who in the Wilderness Years…and how I lived through it.

***** An engaging and enjoyable insight into a fan discovering Doctor Who during the wilderness years

***** A very passionate account of one fans discovery of the greatest science fiction of all time.

**** Perfect for fans of the Doctor in any of his or her forms.

Available from all good book shops.

The Man In The Corner

ISBN: 978-1500549862

A mysterious assassin wants out of his life as a cold and ruthless killer but must face one last assignment before he flicks the escape switch. As he closes in on the biggest criminal mind in the country, he is reminded of what he left behind and how getting closer to the light at the end of the tunnel might also reunite him with a person from his long and distant past. Who is the Big Chief? Why must he be brought down and will it be the end, not just for himself and his superior, but also to the only link to the life he has lost.

***** An exciting book! Whilst focusing on the dark story of an unnamed man, you find yourself sucked into a city of criminals. The chapters contain their own stories which really draw you in and make you want to read more. Great read! The only negative is that it was over too fast.

***** Brilliant read. Did not want to put the book down.

*** This book is a great little read about the path to redemption; not too long, in fact in some places I found myself wishing it might go on a little longer. It's got a sort of style all its own.

Available from all good book shops.

Hayden Gribble was born in Cambridge in June 1989. He has always loved writing and released his debut novel, The Man In The Corner, as an ebook in 2013 before it went paperback the following year.

Captain Random and the Eater of Souls is his fifth book.

Away from writing, Hayden loves reading, walking, sports, music, film and TV.

He has also been a regular member of the Diddly Dum Podcast, a show about Doctor Who, since February 2015 and curates his own James Bond podcast, Podcasters Royale. Both can be found on iTunes.

He lives with his wife in Suffolk.

www.ingramcontent.com/pod-product-compliance
Lightning Source LLC
Chambersburg PA
CBHW060410080526
44583CB00012B/521